KU-733-810

This book is
the last

BULLDOZERS

Shetland Library

Sam Sargent and Michael Alves
629.225
Bulldozers

SHETLAND LIBRARY

91233094

Sam Sargent and Michael Alves

Motorbooks International
Publishers & Wholesalers

Dedication

This book is for Mary, Barbara, and Rachel, our dozer babes.

First published in 1994 by Motorbooks International Publishers & Wholesalers, PO Box 2, 729 Prospect Avenue, Osceola, WI 54020 USA

© Sam Sargent and Michael Alves, 1994

All rights reserved. With the exception of quoting brief passages for the purpose of review no part of this publication may be reproduced without prior written permission from the Publisher

Motorbooks International is a certified trademark, registered with the United States Patent Office

The information in this book is true and complete to the best of our knowledge. All recommendations are made without any guarantee on the part of the author or Publisher, who also disclaim any liability incurred in connection with the use of this data or specific details

We recognize that some words, model names and designations, for example, mentioned herein are the property of the trademark holder. We use them for identification purposes only. This is not an official publication

Motorbooks International books are also available at discounts in bulk quantity for industrial or sales-promotional use. For details write to Special Sales Manager at the Publisher's address

All photos in this book were taken by Sam Sargent unless otherwise noted. All registered trademarks and trade names are the property of their respective companies. The author reserves all rights to this work not granted to the publisher

Library of Congress Cataloging-in-Publication Data

Sargent, Sam.
    Bulldozers / Sam Sargent, Michael Alves.
        p.   cm. — (Enthusiast color series)
    Includes index.
    ISBN 0-87938-887-0
    1. Bulldozers. 2. Deere & Company. 3. Catepillar Inc. I. Alves, Michael. II. Title. III. Series.
    TA725.A46   1994
    629.225—dc20   93-48647

On the front cover: A mighty Caterpillar D10N pushes a mass of dirt in the course of a day's work.

On the frontispiece: It's easy to track a dozer. This one was headed out for a test drive.

On the title page: A Cat D9L with a single-shank ripper takes on an enormous challenge and is up to the task.

On the back cover: One of about 160 female operating engineers in California, Lisa Honeein regularly works out with a 14-ton Caterpillar D6C at the Union of Operating Engineers' school in Ranchero Murieta, California.

Printed and bound in Hong Kong

Contents

WITHDRAWN

Acknowledgments

The authors wish to thank everyone who contributed to this book, especially: Lee Woodward, Deere & Company; Joycelyn Luster and Marsha Hausser, Caterpillar, Inc.; John Giesfeldt, Nelson & Schmidt / Komatsu Dresser Company; Don Frantz and Eric Orlemann, Historical Construction Equipment Association; James Murray, Kiewit Pacific Company; Bill Larkin and Jerry Allen, Granite Rock; Lyle Miller and Dee Crawford, Rasmusson, Inc.; Sergio Gonzales, Sonoma County Public Works; Steve Stromgren, Operating Engineers Local 3; Captain Frank Childress, US Army, Ft. Irwin NTC; Stan Ghisletta and John Schlesiger, Peterson Equipment Company; George Beltrametti, Stony Point Rock Quarry, Inc.; and Rod Pedersen, California Division of Forestry; and Baron Wolman.

Preface

Every little boy has a fascination with heavy equipment. Some of us never outgrew it. In researching and photographing *Bulldozers*, we had the opportunity to experience firsthand the power of these heavy metal workhorses up close. For some people, climbing onto the track treads and swinging up into the cab of a dozer as the sun breaks the horizon is just the start of another day. For us, it was the experience of a lifetime. Driving a dozer is definitely a power trip.

We traveled to America's heartland to see how dozers rise from molten metal, visiting such cities as Peoria, Illinois, headquarters of Caterpillar, Inc., and Dubuque, Iowa, where John Deere dozers are built. We shot dozers at dawn and dusk and in the dark all over the country. Whenever we drove the freeways, we kept a sharp eye out for dozers at work. A business trip to Hawaii even yielded unexpected but welcome shots of yellow bulldozers working the red earth of cane fields in Kauai. What we found was that wherever there's dirt, there are dozers.

We tried to show a broad range of dozers and how they're used in the field. In this book, you'll see the dozers we saw at work, rest, and retirement. It's a close-up look at some very big blades.

Who Took the "Bull" Out of Bulldozers?

How did "a dose fit for a bull" become "a track-type tractor fitted with a broad steel blade in front, used for removing obstacles and leveling uneven surfaces"?

Well, around 1880, the common usage of "bull-dose" in the United States meant administering a large and efficient dose of any sort of medicine or punishment. If you "bull-dosed" someone, you gave him a severe whipping or coerced or intimidated him in some other way, such as by holding a gun to his head. This must have happened pretty often, because by 1886, with a slight variation in spelling, a "bulldozer" had come to mean both a large-caliber pistol and the person who wielded it. In short, these were people and weapons that got things done in an efficient, if somewhat blunt, manner. Anything that got in their way was leveled. So, naturally, by the late 1800s, "bulldozing" came to mean using brawny force to push over, or through, any obstacle.

It wasn't really until 1930, after the introduction of the "crawler" or "track-type" tractor, that the term bulldozing also came to be commonly associated with the act of earth moving, specifically by using a large, slightly curved, steel blade attached to the front of a tractor to push things around.

And if you want to be technically correct, a "bulldozer" actually only refers to the blade of a track-type tractor, not the combination of the two, but this distinction has blurred with time and usage. It seems the frequent pairing of a front-mounted steel blade on a track-type tractor led to the whole assembly commonly being called a bulldozer.

Actually, no one in the bulldozer business even calls their equipment a bulldozer anymore. They're just called "dozers" by the people who use them, and when they're working, they're "dozing"—which could never be confused with someone taking a light rest or nap.

Chapter 1

A Little History

Left
Diesel engines fueled the birth of more powerful bulldozers such as this mid-thirties Caterpillar Diesel Seventy-Five pulling a three-shank ripper. The "D" in Caterpillar's famous D-series track-type tractors comes from Cat's first diesel V-8. The D17000 engine powered the RD8 tractor, later known just as the dependable Cat D8. *Caterpillar, Inc.*

Above
Following the First World War, the Best Company—which in 1925 merged with the Holt Manufacturing Company to form Caterpillar Tractor Company—introduced a new machine. The year was 1921, and the machine was the advanced-for-its-time, gas-powered, enclosed-cab Best 30 "Tracklayer." It's shown here fitted with a light-duty dozer blade. Constant improvements of these track-type tractors—also called crawlers—by Caterpillar and other manufacturers provided the power and performance needed. *Caterpillar, Inc.*

War means work even in the worst weather.
Removing rubble in bomb-damaged Great Britain
required the services of many lend-lease
shipments, including this Caterpillar D7.
Caterpillar, Inc.

Water Tanks for Mesopotamia

There's an interesting story in the evolution of the crawler tractor—the power behind the bulldozer blade—from hardworking farm vehicle to gun-toting tank.

In September of 1914, engineers from the Holt Manufacturing Company were dispatched to England to demonstrate the capability of Holt's "Caterpillar" crawler tractors to haul artillery and supplies under World War I battlefield conditions. In turn, the British War Department sent an officer to Holt's East Peoria, Illinois, plant to learn what he could about these powerful American machines.

Earlier, Ernest Swinton, a British lieutenant colonel (soon to be credited as the father of the modern tank) had developed the idea of an armored "machine gun destroyer" to help break the deadly stalemate of trench warfare. Upon hearing from military friends of an American farm tractor that could "climb like hell," Swinton convinced British manufacturers to add machine guns and cannons to a radically new type of armored crawler tractor. Prototypes of the new machines were dubbed "Water Tanks for Mesopotamia" both to conceal their military mission and because the new enclosed equipment did bear some resemblance to a tubby water tank.

Used experimentally for the first time in the Battle of the Somme in September 1916, the new tanks were only mildly successful; however, seeing their bullets bounce off the tanks had serious demoralizing effects on the entrenched German troops. Slowly gaining tactical experience, the British eventually were able to use the tank's ability to punch across trench lines decisively in the Battle of Cambrai—forever changing the combatants' bloody trench tactics and even shortening the war, according to some experts. The German army also manufactured a few tanks, but estimates are that throughout the war they were able to put only about twenty into action, with little result.

Although no American-built tractors were employed as armed tanks during World War I, more than 10,000 Caterpillar crawlers saw service on the Allies' side as weapons and equipment carriers. By the end of the war, the peaceful powerhouse called a crawler tractor had found a new role as warrior. In 1918, Swinton himself even visited the Holt factory to pay tribute to what he called " the cradle of the tank."

The "Boss of the Beach" was often an armored tractor driven by a combat engineer. Track-type tractors fitted with bulldozer blades were used on every front in World War II to clear mines, build landing strips, and, in more than one instance, charge an enemy-held position under withering fire. One war correspondent tells the story of a small convoy of crawlers that were badly needed to build a road in a valley far below the mountaintop where they were located. To get them down so that they could build the road, engineers simply rolled the driverless dozers off the edge of the cliff, letting them tumble down the mountainside. According to the correspondent, not one machine was put out of action. If they didn't land on their tracks, the soldiers just pushed them upright. All were driven immediately into duty. *Caterpillar, Inc.*

For more than twenty years, Caterpillar's powerful D9—introduced in 1954—was the company's largest dozer. Its bulldozer blade was raised and lowered by using a cable-and-pulley assembly. *Caterpillar, Inc.*

John Deere dozers carved a construction niche during the boom years of the fifties and sixties. Bulldozers changed the face of America by helping to build millions of miles of roads and leveling the land for every American's dream— a house. *Deere & Company*

Bulldozer Builders

Left
Among them—Dave Rinker, Carl Ballard, Fred Vaughn, and Terry Bode—have more than 113 years of experience building bulldozers for John Deere.

Above
To ensure complete coverage, various parts of the bulldozer are painted separately. A dozer's coiled tracks are shown here as they emerge dripping wet from a paint bath.

The heart of every bulldozer is the engine. Here, Robert Pluemer readies a 550 series engine for mating to a dozer on John Deere's utility crawler tractor assembly line. John Deere's larger dozers are also assembled in the 1.2 mile-long Dubuque, Iowa, manufacturing facility, which has five million square feet of manufacturing space under one roof.

Les Simmons and Benny Martensen lower a large B-series dozer onto its tracks. The massive U-frame assembly is the attachment point for the bulldozer's blade. At John Deere's Dubuque Works, as soon as the crawlers are fully tracked, they are driven to the next assembly area within the 1.2 mile-long plant. In a field operation, putting the tracks on a bulldozer would take at least 30 minutes. On the assembly line, it takes less than 10 minutes.

An 8-ton, G-series bulldozer rides an overhead track on its way to the painting booth. John Deere's standard construction equipment color is yellow, but the company will custom paint any color a customer orders.

A large John Deere 750B crawler is prepped in the painting booth by technician Charlie Leppert. It takes about 6 gallons (gal) of lead-free, "JDMF9LA-Industrial Yellow" to paint the company's smaller G-series dozer.

If One's Good, Two Are Better

If your biggest tractor isn't big enough, what do you do? Well, you might try putting two together. In 1969, that's just what the Caterpillar Tractor Company did with the introduction of the side-by-side SxSD9G and the Quad-Track DD9G. Each of these unique models featured two connected D9G track-type tractors working in sync: The SxS used two tractors coupled together to push a single bulldozer blade; while the Quad-Track put two tractors in tandem—nose to tail—to provide more power to shove a scraper.

Manufactured from 1974-1977, the 92-ton SxSD9H version used two Model D353 six-cylinder, four-stroke diesel engines—each with a displacement of 1,473ci—to develop a total of 820hp. The two tractors were connected at three points: at the rear with a 16in-diameter structural-steel tubular tie bar; in the center with a box-construction brace between the track frames; and at the front by the 7ft, 2in high, 24ft long bulldozer blade. The whole machine was operated by one person from the left tractor. In a turn, power was supplied to three of the four tracks. The two units could also be separated and run individually if needed.
Photo copyright by Eric Orlemann

Harnessing the power of two D9H tractors was the 770hp DD9G (which was replaced in 1974 by the DD9H). Although the entire Quad-Track arrangement was discontinued by Caterpillar after 1980, several examples are still working in the US. Dual controls allow the joined unit to be operated by one person from either machine, or the pair can

be disconnected and used as two single tractors. Only the lead tractor came fitted with a bulldozer blade; a blade and hydraulic control were available as optional equipment for the rear tractor. The approximate shipping weight for the DD9G was 175,000lb, about 87.5 tons. *Photo copyright by Eric Orlemann*

Chapter 3

School of Hard Rocks

In the small town of Rancho Murieta, California, Local 3 of the Union of Operating Engineers runs an annual apprenticeship training program for students from forty-six northern California counties. Annually, the 23-year-old program teaches approximately 150 people the fine art and subtle skills of operating heavy equipment. No experience is necessary. A written application is all that it takes to apply. Housed and fed by the union for the first five weeks of the program, hopeful dozer apprentices start out by learning the basics of earth moving—grade setting, cutting, and filling. By the time they receive a certificate of completion, they've spent more than 6,400hr of operating time in the driver's seat. Although wages vary by location, experience, and company, northern California bulldozer operators average about $24 per hour. With benefits, the total compensation package adds up to about $45 per hour. Steady work depends on the cconomy.

Left
With his dozer's back-up beeper blaring, David Floyd of Cotati, California, rips neatly through the edge of a bluff during a day of training on a D6D. He's a "Stage 4" operator, with nearly enough hours to earn his certificate.

Driving a Dozer Isn't What It Seems

At first glance, you'd think driving a dozer was easy. It's not. But if you ask just about anybody who runs one for a living, their first dozer experience came when they were still in their tender teens. It seems age 12 is the perfect time to begin driving dozers—oops, *operating* dozers; "Teamsters *drive*, operating engineers *operate*," according to dozer instructor Deane Sweet, the man who put me at the controls of a Caterpillar D4H.

Most people who make a career out of operating heavy equipment started by growing up using large pieces of machinery like dozers "down on the farm" early in their lives. They're comfortable making machines respond to their commands—commands like go, stop, turn, don't run over that. It's basic stuff, but there's hardly anybody who's a smooth dozer operator right off the bat. This is a skill that takes time to develop.

The first thing is, you don't just put the blade down and go. That's not to say you can't, but if you have the ambition to cut a nice, level road without camel-sized humps, it would help to develop the eye-hand-foot coordination of Joe Montana before you try to do it with a dozer.

Dozers are big, and you can't actually see what you're pushing with that blade out front. You've got to "feel" the steel respond to pressure, watch how much dirt is spilling off the side of the blade, and constantly make small adjustments. Generally, the blade controls are to your right, and the track controls are to your left. You decelerate the dozer's engine by pushing the throttle lever down with your right foot. If it operated like a car (down for fast), you couldn't hold the pedal down after a long day of bouncing around in a dozer cab. You brake with your left foot.

The D4H I used was equipped with a "six-way" blade, that is, you could position it up or down, tilt it left or right, or angle it either direction using a single lever on the right of the driver's seat. The track controls use two levers, one for each track. If you pull up on the left lever just a little, the left track slows and you begin slowly turning left. If you pull the lever farther back, the track locks and you make a very hard left-hand swing. (You can almost turn a dozer in its own length this way.) To move, you just take your foot off the decelerator and switch between the two track levers, depending on which way you want to go and how fast you want to turn. Shifting into reverse requires throwing a third lever.

After giving me a brief explanation of the controls and showing me how to use the two-way radio all dozer trainees wear to get instructions—and warning me that the rollover protection system was good for only one roll—Sweet retreated to the safety of his van as I fired up my D4 and headed out for my first try at pushing a little dirt around the union's training site at Rancho Murieta.

Actually, I wasn't bad; Sweet says he's seen worse. (Nice of him to say that.)

I swung the high-tracked D4H around a big old D8H and proceeded to make a nice, straight pass with the blade cutting turned-up soil about a foot deep. So much for beginner's luck.

On my next pass, I tried to dig a little deeper. Then it happened. I got behind the machine. As I lowered the blade, the dozer pitched down and slowed down. To compensate, I raised the blade. That got me back to speed, but now my blade was too high. So I lowered it. It dug in. I slowed down. So I raised it... well, you can guess the rest.

As I looked back at the roller coaster road I'd just created, I vowed never to waste my money renting a bulldozer I planned to use myself. It's a power trip, but if I need something done with a dozer, I'll leave operating it to an operating engineer.

Fifty-eight-year-old Deane Sweet has been teaching the techniques of bulldozer operation at Rancho Murieta for the past seven years. He started running dozers when he was 12. At one point in his career, to finish a job, he ran a dozer twenty-four straight hours without taking a break. Dozer instructors and students are linked by radio so that the secrets of such smooth operators as Deane Sweet can be passed on more efficiently. Experienced instructors can tell right away if someone has potential; a few who don't have the necessary eye-hand-foot coordination, depth perception, and patience to learn the trade get washed out every year.

Formerly the site of an old placer gold mine, the union's 80-acre training area is now part of a sprawling ranch. Large cuts in the gently rolling hills were carved by miners using water cannons during the 1800s. In a mutually beneficial deal, the rancher who owns the land lets the union's dozer operators train there in return for restoring the site to a more natural configuration.

33

Lisa Honeein has what it takes to make a fine dozer operator, according to Deane Sweet, her instructor. The Santa Cruz resident grew up operating farm equipment.

One of about 160 female operating engineers in California, Lisa Honeein regularly works out with a 14-ton Caterpillar D6C at the union's school.

The beginning of another long day at dozer school is just the start of this operating engineer's career. The union offers training in a wide variety of heavy equipment.

Chapter 4

Big Deals

Left
Paul Smith flew out to Turlock, California from Wauconda, Illinois, to test drive this used Caterpillar D5H LGP for his brother's excavating firm. With about 1,500 operating hours on the engine—which Smith considers about a year's worth of work in Illinois—this dozer is on the market for $77,000. Brand new, it cost around $150,000. Publications such as *Rock & Dirt,* published in Crossville, Tennessee, help buyers and sellers of heavy equipment find each other.

Above
The wider-track shoes and longer undercarriage help this Caterpillar dozer work especially well in soft ground. The distinctive tracks are self-cleaning Apex mud pads that don't pick up as much muck. Smith put the dozer through its paces by digging a 5ft hole in United Equipment's test track and filling it back in, working the Cat crawler into tight angles and moving loads of dirt to shake out any potential problems in the used machine. After a 30min test drive, he was ready to deal.

Redwood tread substitutes for steel track on this one-of-a-kind, "walk-in" bulldozer. The building's architect, Cliff Cheney, included steel shift levers on the roof of the two-story bulldozer to lend even more authenticity to the design. It's got to be the only dozer with a permanent street address.

You can't miss United Equipment's building along busy Highway 99 in the small town of Turlock, California. Built in 1976 by the company's owner, Harold Logsdon, the 21ft-high, 28ft-wide, 66ft-long, realistic looking bulldozer is made from redwood and plywood. Complete with steel and aluminum hydraulics, it houses the firm's sales offices. That's a 7ft-tall Cat D4D parked in front of the building. If this wooden bulldozer had an engine, it could push a load much bigger than the 6ft-high mound of sand and rocks piled in front.

This old D8H uses a cable-and-pulley assembly
to raise and lower the blade. Like wrinkled skin,
the well-worn blade testifies to long years of hard
work in the sun. Today, a comparable, fresh-from-
the-factory D8H would cost about $350,000.

Dozers: Facts and Figures

How Many Bulldozers are There in the US?

Equipment Data Associates estimates that at any one time, there are about 116,000 operating dozers in America. Forty-three percent of this fleet—that's about 50,000 bulldozers—were purchased new between 1987 and 1992.

Building, highway, and heavy construction firms own approximately 60 percent of all operating bulldozers in the US, but mining and materials firms bought 30 percent of all new dozers.

How Long Do Dozers Last?

According to a survey by *Construction Equipment* magazine, this is how it breaks out.

Average hours at retirement for different size dozers:

Under 100hp	12,000
100 to 200hp	16,500
More than 200hp	19,500

It's obvious that bigger dozers live longer.

Average annual operating hours for different dozer owners:

Building Contractors	1,130
Highway/heavy Contractors	1,290
General Heavy Contractors	1,430
Materials Producers	2,500
Utilities	1,040
Mining	2,760
Government	740
Other Non-Construction	1,250

Perhaps the President might put those low-hour government dozers to work in Washington, D.C. Getting a bill pushed through Congress could definitely be done a lot quicker from the seat of a bulldozer.

How Much Does a Dozer Cost?

According to estimates compiled by Equipment Data Associates, expect to pay around $78,000 for a new 100hp machine. If you want something in the 500hp range, you'll pay about $370,000. A new D11N will set you back nearly $900,000.

Most people buy this type of equipment. In 1991, only 9 percent of dozer users rented; however, that's triple the number of renters there were in 1987, according to one study.

What's the world's biggest dozer?

The Komatsu 575A-2 earns that honor. It has a 1050hp engine and tips the scales at 291,010lb.

What's the largest American-made dozer?

Caterpillar's D11N weighs 214,847 lb and rolls along courtesy of a 770hp V-8 engine. It's built in Peoria, Illinois.

Chapter 5

Fire Fighter

Left
Former F-14 Navy Fighter Pilot Gary Beverlin dons a fireproof, cloth-lined, communications-equipped racing helmet modified with a filtered air breathing system for close-in fire fighting with his Fiat-Allis HD-11EP dozer. In this machine, Beverlin, a California Division of Forestry (CDF) heavy fire equipment operator, can work smoke-shrouded hills with grades as steep as 70 percent. The formerly stock tractor received a CARCO F-50 winch, full ROPS (Roll-Over Protection Structure), brush screens, dust filter, belly guards, an extra set of side-mounted lights, and several other modifications by the CDF before it qualified as a fire fighter. It sports a 12ft, 6in-long manual angle and tilt blade.

Above
Since Beverlin's dozer is part of an "initial response unit," rolling to every CDF fire call in the dry hills north of Healdsburg, California, speed is important. Beverlin routinely has the 43,000-lb HD-11EP unchained, fired up, and off the Fruehauf Tilt-Top trailer within 3-5min of arriving at a blaze. The trailer actually performs a balancing act. Unlocked but not unhitched, it splits in the middle as the weight of the tractor shifts, allowing the dozer to back directly onto the ground. To avoid "wide-load" road requirements while en route to the fire, the dozer's blade is set at a 45 degree angle to minimize its width. The entire setup is towed by the CDF's 1980 GMC Brigadier dual-axle truck.

The upside-down license plate is an "in" joke among CDF dozer crews. Another dozer driver had a similar upside-down plate, one he mounted inside a license plate holder with the inscription "If you can read this, turn me over." Fortunately, Beverlin has never rolled his dozer while on the job, but his HD-11EP's ROPS is certified for up to three rolls before requiring reinspection. Notice the two canteens and extra set of backup lights above the winch.

The CDF protects its dozer operators in a variety of ways. Beverlin's HD-11EP is outfitted with roll-down, reflective aluminum fire curtains on three sides of the cab. He breathes filtered—but not cooled—air through his helmet. The air is scrubbed of smoke and pesticide residue by charcoal filters inside the 3M-built agricultural air filtration unit shown behind his right shoulder. The helmet is also fitted with a communications microphone and earphones. In the upper right of the cab is an eighty-channel Midland radio that Beverlin uses to stay in touch with various other firefighters, including those flying air tankers. If the dozer is about to be overrun by swiftly moving flames, the operator can signal for an air drop of fire retardant on his bulldozer in one of two ways. He can either call in a tanker on the radio, or by turning on the aircraft strobe beacon light mounted in the roof of the dozer's cab. If that fails, the only things left are the cab's heat shields, a portable fire extinguisher, a protective fire blanket, and the burn kit that every dozer driver carries.

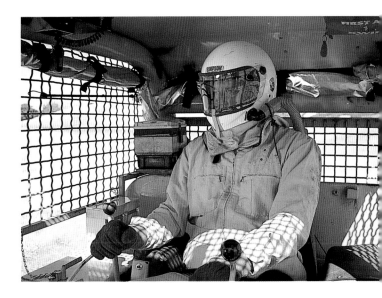

Immediately after the liberation of Kuwait during the 1991 Gulf War, Caterpillar D8Ns and D9Ns were used to help put out hundreds of oil well fires. *Caterpillar, Inc.*

Chapter 6

Road Builder

Left
Near Cloverdale, California, a Cat D9L with a single-shank ripper starts a day's work on a freeway bypass around the city. C. A. Rasmusson contractors blasted a mountain of rock for the Highway 101 bypass, then used dozers to move it.

Above
Two of Kiewit Pacific Construction's Caterpillar D10 dozers team up to push a scraper leveling a roadbed under construction near Hayward, California.

A Kiewit Pacific CAT D9N dozer rips the bed for a new super-highway in California. Mounted on the rear of the tractor is a hydraulically operated, twin-shank parallelogram ripper that can cut nearly 32in deep, with a penetration force of nearly 33,000lb. Once the dirt is loosened, a scraper can scoop it up and transport it. Notice the Cat tractor's unique elevated sprocket undercarriage. According to Caterpillar, this design helps to increase traction and reduce maintenance.

Working with almost choreographed precision, four Caterpillar crawlers move in a veritable bulldozer ballet. Two dozers push a scraper as it piles up a load of soil, while two others rip the ground, loosening the dirt for the next scraper pass. Millions of tons of earth are moved from the construction site this way.

A protruding hard point on the rear of the scraper, called a "stinger," is what the dozer's blade pushes against. It's usually slathered in grease to protect against metal-on-metal wear.

Neither rock nor dirt stands in the way of a determined dozer driver. This D9L operator pushes a massive load down what is to become a California freeway.

Rectangular steel "wear plates" are welded to the sides of this dozer's Beales-manufactured blade. Abrasive materials such as rock then wear out the wear plates—which can be easily replaced—instead of the blade.

Sporting a huge "slope board" like an outstretched arm, a Cat D9L outfitted with a single-shank ripper heads for the hills. Various-sized slope boards are used for grading angles on hills. They're mounted on the side of the dozer, and raised or lowered hydraulically so that the bulldozer can cut a slope or terrace without making a steep traverse across the hill.

This Cat D10N is using a short, side-mounted grading blade to cut an angle. With various attachments, the bulldozer becomes a versatile earthmover that can shape the landscape to exacting specifications.

Next page
Bulldozer work is often needed even after a road is built. To keep from tearing up the road, this CASE-built 550E uses a steel-corded rubber track instead of a traditional metal track. *J. I. Case Company*

A Cat D3 dozer driver adjusts the angle of a spade nose blade used for cutting small trenches. It's unique attachments like these that let bulky bulldozers move and reshape the ground exactly as planners and developers desire.

A single pass with a spade nose blade quickly cuts a neat furrow between the little D3's tracks.

Caterpillar's most massive dozer is the D11N. It's 14ft, 11in tall, 12ft wide, and sports a 37,239lb, 8ft-high, 20ft-long U-blade with a capacity of 45 yards of material. It weighs in at 214, 847lb with full fuel and a single-shank ripper. A four-stroke, 770hp V-8 engine with a 388gal diesel fuel tank keeps the D11N going. Optional equipment includes both a 161lb air conditioner and a 450lb "Arctic package." Base price is a little more than $890,000. *Photo copyright by Eric Orlemann*

Chapter 7

Rock Crusher

Who Are These Guys?

It seems as if every bulldozer operator we met while researching this book was cut from similar cloth. As a group, they were straight-talking, no-nonsense, firm-hand-shake, likeable guys who started driving dozers down on the farm. And generally, they exuded energy.

We met guys like 69-year-old Buck Piazza of Penngrove, California, who leaped down from his dozer's 10ft-high cab in one step when we asked to take his picture. "Anything I can do. Where do you want it?" said Piazza, helpfully. When we asked him to run the dozer up the side of a huge boulder and pound away at the seemingly solid rock, he obliged without a moment's hesitation, churning his huge D9L up a slippery slope to plow away pieces for a photo.

In other chapters of this book, you'll read about guys like Mike Pieper, an Iowa farmer we met as he worked round-the-clock to build a pumping station to drain 14,000 acres of flooded farmland. Unable to drive our car along the soggy levee to the construction site, we hitched a ride on Pieper's Honda all-terrain vehicle—the three of us barreling along the top of the dike on a bike built for one. To get back to the road after taking pictures, Pieper's cousin Carl fired up a small skiff and boated us over the family farm, ruined by a 48hr flood of Mississippi River mud and water. It was the kind of devastation that would crush lesser men. But to men like Pieper, it was just another obstacle to overcome, a job that needed to be done—and that's what a dozer does best.

As one British officer in World War II said after meeting bulldozer operators, "Most of them are damned fools about their machines. They have utterly no fear, drive the things everywhere nonchalantly, and get mad as the devil if shells or bullets hit their beloved machines...they all chew tobacco, swear magnificently, never bathe, and are so very adept at repair that it is a matter of pride with them not to ask repair crews for help."

A Komatsu bulldozer cuts a quarry terrace. Pushing a mass of rock and dirt before it, the dozer cuts into the hill to create a shelf from which to work. Somebody's got to be the first one to carve his way up or down a slope, and no one's better equipped than a man with a bulldozer.

With the early morning sun rising behind him, 69-year-old Buck Piazza of Penngrove, California, fires up his Caterpillar D9L for another day of making big rocks into little ones. Rock crushing operations are wonderful examples of what happens when an immovable object meets an irresistible force—like a 100,000lb Cat crawler. With his Cat tractor's massive ripper poised like some deadly giant claw, Piazza attacks his quarry head on...

Buck gets a blade full...

To all the dozer operators who posed for our pictures, thank you. You bring to mind a famous phrase uttered in a movie about Butch Cassidy and the Sundance Kid. In scene after scene, Butch and Sundance are relentlessly pursued by Pinkerton agents bent on their arrest. No matter what they do, Butch and Sundance can't shake the agents. Each time Butch looks back at the tireless, rugged riders bearing down on them, he says "Who *are* those guys?" They're guys who didn't give up, didn't give in, and just did their job...just like you.

...gives a little shove...and turns another rock into a rock pile. Of course, his "little shove" could probably level a house.

A large part of the quarry business is separating the good rocks from the bad. Here, a dozer operator slices a path between mounds of sorted rock.

Dick Carber works for Wendling Quarries, Inc., in Dewitt, Iowa. He's put in thirty years of "hard time" breaking rocks in the quarry business. He casually switches between driving different types of equipment the way most people switch between using a knife and fork.

Working in a portable quarry operation between Ft. Madison and Burlington, Iowa, Dick Carber spends a good part of his day pushing piles of rocks around with a well-worn Caterpillar D7 equipped with a Carco TD-18 winch manufactured in 1957.

Next page
Perched precariously on the lip of a quarry shelf, this Komatsu-made bulldozer has just finished shoving a load of rocks over the side. Tanker trucks continually spray water, which helps keep down the dust churned up by these machines. A skilled bulldozer operator, ever at risk of going over the lip, hopes never to put his dozer's rollover protection system to the test. A simple lap belt holds him to his seat.

Above
A massive, reinforced bulldozer blade attached to an equally massive machine such as this Komatsu dozer literally moves mountains. Notice that the machine's high-mounted headlights are on; this helps the driver see in the dim light and dusty air of the quarry.

Next page
The Komatsu 575A-2 is the world's largest bulldozer. It weighs 291,010lb and uses a 1050hp V-12 engine to push a giant 70yd-capacity, high-tensile strength, steel U-dozer blade. The operator's cab is mounted on rubber shock absorbers. *Komatsu Dresser Company*

Working to rebuild the broken Green Bay Bottom levee surrounding his 3,200-acre farm, Mike Pieper slogs through the thick Mississippi River mud in a Caterpillar D6C equipped with extra lights, a full ROPS, Hyster W6EC winch, and Balderson blade. The dozer's wide track helps spread its weight and keeps it from sinking into soft surfaces such as this mud.

With water over his entire farm, Mike Pieper can't help but get his Cat tractor's feet wet. He put in 18-hour days to build a pumping station he designed to drain the area flooded by the levee breaks.

Like the proverbial postman who can't be stopped by mud, rain, sleet, or snow, this Cat D6C undercarriage delivers under the toughest of conditions.

72

Previous page
A John Deere 850B Long Track and a Caterpillar
D5B take a short rest from round-the-clock work
in a Hawaiian sugar cane field. The red soil is a
product of Hawaii's volcanic origin.

Above
Equipped with a specialized curved rake with
springs, this Cat D5B has been modified to sweep
up piles of sugar cane on the island of Kauai.

Next page
Seen from the air, four bulldozers and
accompanying scrapers carve out a new vineyard
in the rolling hills north of Healdsburg, California.
Unequaled in its ability to change the lay of the
land, the bulldozer plays an important part in
agricultural operations all over the world.

Previous page
Thousands of acres of sugar cane, a crop once harvested by many people and horses, begin the trip to your table, courtesy of one man and his machine.

Down on the farm, if you need it now, you build it. Here, a hitching bracket is welded to the back of a Caterpillar D9 ripper assembly.

Sixty-one-year-old Tom Burger of Yorkville, California, catches a little rest between farm and logging jobs with his old Cat D7 and 1941-vintage Hyster winch. He has driven dozers since he was 12 and has a simple philosophy: "You just get on and run them."

Sometimes field repairs are necessary. In a vineyard outside of Healdsburg, California, the mechanics working on this D9G have it made in the shade.

This Cat D7 has traded its blade for an unusual spaded rake attachment used for plowing down thick stalks of cane. The operator wears a mask to filter out dust and smoke—notice the fire extinguisher—which billows up during the harvesting operation.

What you see is what you get—in this case, a Cat D7. The solid steel specifications plate is as sturdy as the machine. A tin plate like those found on cars would never do on a dozer.

Just outside the little town of Dickson Mounds, Illinois, a John Deere JD 450 gets tucked away at the end of the day in a bed of rolled bales of hay.

Chapter 9

Landfill Load

Left
Pushing a ton of trash before it, a Caterpillar tractor makes room for more at the Sonoma County, California, sanitary landfill. The extra catch-guard extending above the blade keeps trash from rolling over the top and piling up in front of the tractor.

Above
Sanitary landfills are made sanitary by alternating layers of dirt and garbage. This old Cat D9N is used to rip up the soil and push it into piles to be picked up by a scraper.

To get a full load of dirt, rubber-tired scrapers often require a little push from their beefy bulldozer brothers.

Previous page
Seemingly oblivious to the monster machine at work beside it, a neatly camouflaged sea gull scans Sonoma County's rubbish for its next meal. Note the clothing and other garbage caught up amidst the treads. Garbage is on a fast track with this dozer.

More Glamorous Jobs: Dozers in the Movies

Dozens of dozers have had featured parts in movies. Who can forget the classic *Fighting Seabees* with none other than John Wayne playing the part of a heroic dozer driver who, under a hail of sniper bullets, saves the day by driving his dozer into a gas tank to torch attacking tanks? (If you haven't seen it, don't worry. Nobody kills The Duke. It's just a flesh wound.)

Mel Gibson rampaged through a housing tract with bullets bouncing off the blade of his bulldozer in a *Lethal Weapon* flick. It just shows that it doesn't pay to get in the way of a mad Australian road warrior with a loaded dozer.

Some of the other movies featuring dozers: The sci-fi *Tremors* featured Kevin Bacon and Fred Ward rumbling across the desert in a dozer to escape a mutant killer worm—a very big one, of course. *Vanishing Point* ended with a drug-dazed driver running his car straight into a dozer roadblock at about 100mph. The infamous *Killdozer*, filmed in 1974, saw a deadly dozer with a mind of its own try to do in Clint Walker, Robert Urich, and an entire construction crew.

If you can round them up, these movies would make a great night of down and dirty dozer action on your VCR at home.

While it looks like it might be ready for the scrap
heap itself, this well-worn Caterpillar D6C is just
getting an overhaul. Within a few days,
mechanics had it back on the job at the landfill.

Chapter 10

Armored Blades

The Dozer Wages War.

Militarized dozers have seen plenty of action, from Pacific beaches in World War II all the way to the shifting sands of the Saudi Arabian desert during the crises in the Gulf. In war paint, this versatile machine has been called on to level everything from landing strips to land mines. Its role was so key in World War II that legendary tank commander General George Patton once said that if he were forced to choose between using tanks and bulldozers for an invasion, he'd take dozers every time.

Stories of dozer drivers overcoming insurmountable obstacles to achieve their objectives are legendary. Here are just a few of them.

An 88,000lb D8N gets a lift directly from Caterpillar's headquarters in Peoria, Illinois, to Kuwait via a giant C-5A military transport. In the aftermath of the Gulf War, many machines like this were equipped with fire-fighting capabilities and rushed overseas to help put out the oil well fires started by Iraq's retreating army. *Caterpillar, Inc.*

Normandy—Putting a Pillbox out of Action

Faced with withering fire from a German pillbox—a low, concrete bunker filled with machine guns—during the invasion of Normandy, British Royal Engineers trundled a dozer around to a "blind spot" in back of the beach-front fortification. There, they dropped the blade on their dozer and began pushing a mound of earth, angling it into the firing slits cut in the side of the enemy-held machine gun nest. One by one, each slit was smothered, and each gun silenced, opening a bullet-free path for British soldiers to advance up the beach.

Kuwait—Filling a Trench

The Iraqi army that invaded Kuwait dug deeply fortified trenches and awaited the inevitable assault by Allied armored forces. But they didn't count on the ingenuity of US engineers. Avoiding a frontal attack, tanks fitted with earth-moving blades swung parallel to the trench line, one on either side of the enemy. As they held down the entrenched troops with machine gun fire, the tanks lowered their blades and plowed slowly, steadily

In the high desert of the Army's Ft. Irwin National Training Center outside Barstow, California, 19-year-old Specialist Brad Kincaid of Kentucky puts a 19-ton M-9 ACE (Armored Combat Earthmover) from the 1st Cavalry Division, 91st Engineers Battalion, into action. His unit is based in Killeen, Texas. Designed to keep up with the Army's fast tanks and armored troop transports, the unarmed ACE rolls along at a top speed of 37 miles per hour (mph). A 260hp Cummins 903 engine provides the power. Before dozing, the entire vehicle dips at the nose and the ACE's hinged blade opens to scoop up an additional 1.5 ton of dirt in a unique central cavity. The added weight increases traction and the dirt is dumped before travel. The vehicle's one-person crew is protected by a 3/8in-thick armor plate.

ahead, filling the trench with tons of earth and burying any opposition.

"Vera," the Battlefield Bulldozer

Advancing right behind the first wave of infantry, in the face of shrapnel from shells and mortars during an attack on a German-held position during World War II, Corporal J. B. Hillsdon of the Royal Engineers cleverly used his bulldozer's bulk to protect him while he worked. After lowering the blade and setting the controls for slow forward, he and his crewman jumped off their beloved "Vera" (they also called their machine "The Rolling Stone") and huddled behind her as she cut a path for the tanks and armored vehicles to follow, pelted by bullets and bombs. An accompanying infantry officer was so impressed that he inquired if this unmanned bulldozer was actually a robot.

Praised by general and infantry joe alike, the bulldozer has earned a well-deserved reputation as an indispensable piece of military equipment. As one World War II serviceman put it, "They could have sent us all the airplanes in the world, but if they hadn't sent us bulldozers, too, we might as well have stayed home."

If it has to, the ACE can even float across a stream with the addition of a strapped-on rubber collar. The tracks double as paddles.

Although not primarily designed for dozing dirt, the M-88 Recovery Vehicle is fitted with a bulldozer blade for pushing vehicles and debris out of the way. Its main job is towing tanks.

The most heavily armed dirt digger in the U.S. Army's arsenal is the M1A1 tank. Fitted with a mine plow, the tank pushes through the ground at a speed of 8 to 10mph while burrowing up lethal mines. The plow is manually lowered to one of three pre-set depths by a cable controlled by the tank's driver. It is retracted by two electric motors.

There's not much that can stop this tank. In the Gulf War, even direct hits by Iraq's T-72 tanks just bounced off the M1A1's armor.

Gunner Tim Thomas, Vehicle Commander Donald Quinn, Driver Jeffrey DeRosa, and Loader Dwaine Randall crew this CEV (Combat Engineer Vehicle). Here, they take a short break before an after-action review of a training exercise at Ft. Irwin. Capable of defending itself if necessary, this armored dozer carries a 50 caliber M-85 machine gun in the top turret and a 7.62-millimeter (mm) M-240 machine gun in the main turret. It fires a 65lb charge of C4 plastic explosive from its large 165mm demolition gun. The charge bursts upon impact to blow up obstacles the CEV can't push out of the way. Top speed for the 57.5-ton vehicle is about 35mph; it averages 15-20mph in cross-country travel.

To make the training battlefield seem more realistic, Ft. Irwin's 1000sq mi of desert include several well-shot-up wrecks. To clear a path for smaller vehicles during a battle against the base's resident OPFOR (Opposing Force), this CEV uses its blade to push one of these blasted hulks out of the way. The vehicle's boom can lift up to 35,000lb and it can tow nearly 50,000lb.

SHETLAND LIBRARY

Index